DOGS SET VII

COCKAPOOS

Jill C. Wheeler
ABDO Publishing Company

visit us at
www.abdopublishing.com

Published by ABDO Publishing Company, 8000 West 78th Street, Edina, Minnesota 55439. Copyright © 2008 by Abdo Consulting Group, Inc. International copyrights reserved in all countries. No part of this book may be reproduced in any form without written permission from the publisher. The Checkerboard Library™ is a trademark and logo of ABDO Publishing Company.

Printed in the United States.

Cover Photo: Chelle Rohde Calbert/www.designerdoggies.com
Interior Photos: Alamy pp. 6, 7, 9, 11, 13, 14, 21; AP Images p. 15; Chelle Rohde
    Calbert/www.designerdoggies.com p. 5; iStockphoto pp. 17, 19

Editors: Tamara L. Britton, Heidi M.D. Elston
Art Direction: Neil Klinepier

Library of Congress Cataloging-in-Publication Data

Wheeler, Jill C., 1964-
  Cockapoos / Jill C. Wheeler.
      p. cm. -- (Dogs. Set VII)
  Includes index.
  ISBN 978-1-59928-962-5
  1. Cockapoo--Juvenile literature. I. Title.

  SF429.C54W44 2008
  636.72--dc22
                              2007031519

CONTENTS

Building a Better Dog

There are hundreds of dog **breeds** to choose from. Each breed is distinctive. Each has a different personality and different habits.

This wide array of breeds is the result of years of work. In fact, humans have been living with dogs for about 12,000 years. Modern dogs began when ancient peoples trained wolf pups to help them hunt. Dogs and wolves are part of the Canidae **family**.

Even with so many breeds to choose from, some people still can't find the perfect dog. That is where designer dogs come in. Designer dogs are created by **breeding** two different **purebred** dogs. Cockapoos blend the qualities of the poodle with those of the cocker spaniel.

The cockapoo is possibly the perfect pet!

COCKER SPANIELS

The cocker spaniel is the smallest member of the sporting dog group. People began breeding "Spanyells" in the 1300s. Cocker spaniels got their name from their skillful hunting of the woodcock, a popular **game** bird. The **American Kennel Club (AKC)** recognized the breed in 1878. In 1892, England's Kennel Club recognized the breed. In 1946, the AKC recognized two separate breeds, the English cocker spaniel and the American cocker spaniel.

An English cocker spaniel

6

Today, the American cocker spaniel is one of the most popular dog **breeds** in the United States. Cockers are easily recognized by their floppy, curly-haired ears and long, silky coat.

They are quick-witted and intelligent. That makes them easier to train and housebreak than some other breeds. Cockers are sweet, loyal, and cheerful. These calm dogs make the perfect family pet!

An American cocker spaniel

POODLES

The poodle **breed** began hundreds of years ago as a working dog. Poodles worked with hunters, recovering **game** from water. In fact, the name poodle comes from the German word for puddle!

In the 1500s, French and German breeders continued to develop the poodle. They chose the most skilled poodles for breeding in order to produce an ever-better hunting dog.

Years of selective breeding created three sizes of poodle. Standard poodles are the largest. Next in size are miniature poodles. Toy poodles are the smallest.

The **AKC** first recognized poodles in 1887. Today, poodles are among the world's most popular pets. Only seven other breeds have more AKC registrations than the poodle.

Poodles are smart and easy to train. Their intelligence and willingness to please make them natural performers. Poodles are also good with children and other pets. It is easy to see why people love them.

The poodle's haircut comes from its working days. The shaved areas helped the dog swim more easily, and the unshaved hair protected its internal organs from cold water.

THE COCKAPOO STORY

Cockapoos have been **bred** since the 1950s. Most people believe the first cockapoos were unplanned. Yet people loved the sweet, patient dogs that resulted from breeding a poodle with a cocker spaniel. Cockapoos made wonderful family pets.

There are two different kinds of cockapoos. The American cockapoo is a cross between a poodle and an American cocker spaniel. The English cockapoo is a cross between a poodle and an English cocker spaniel.

Most cockapoos have a poodle parent and a cocker spaniel parent. But, some cockapoos have

two cockapoo parents. However, American and English cocker spaniels are two different **breeds**. For that reason, an American cockapoo should not be bred with an English cockapoo.

In some countries, cockapoos are known as spoodles.

COCKAPOOS

Most cockapoo **breeders** aim for a dog that does not look like either of its parents. Instead, they want a **unique** cockapoo look.

The cockapoo has medium to long ears and large, round brown eyes. The body is compact and well balanced, with a tail that is either straight or curled.

The coat should be long and full all over, including on the legs and the **muzzle**. Hair around the eyes should be trimmed so it does not affect the dog's vision.

In addition to a specific look, cockapoo breeders seek a healthy dog. **Purebred** dogs often suffer from inherited health problems. If a puppy's mother and father have a condition, the puppy may get it, too.

Some breeders hope that the AKC will recognize the cockapoo breed.

Crossing two different **purebred** dogs introduces different genes to their puppies. This lowers a puppy's chance of inheriting a health problem. The genes a puppy will inherit cannot be known. However, good cockapoo **breeders** choose only the healthiest parents for their cockapoos.

BEHAVIOR

Many people choose cockapoos because they want a **mellow** but smart dog. For that, cockapoos do not disappoint! They are friendly, loving, and eager to please. Cockapoos are generally well behaved around children. They also are good around other pets, especially if they first meet when the cockapoos are puppies.

Unlike their parent breeds, cockapoos do not make good hunting dogs!

Normally, cockapoos are quiet dogs. However, they may bark if they are left alone. This is because they prefer to be around people.

Training is important for cockapoos. An early focus on training leads to a lifetime of good behavior. Some people train cockapoos to work as therapy dogs. Their friendly nature and low-shedding coats make them perfect for the job.

Cockapoos love being a part of family activities!

COATS & COLORS

The poodle contributes much to the cockapoo's popularity. Many dogs have fur that grows to a certain length, then falls out. This is called shedding.

But the poodle coat grows long, much like human hair. That means poodles shed less than most dogs. Cockapoos that inherit this gene are a good choice for people who are allergic to dog fur and **dander**.

Cockapoo hair can be curly, wavy, or flat. It can grow long, but it should be trimmed from time to time. Cockapoos need daily grooming to remove loose hair and prevent snarls. Cockapoos can be many colors. These include black, white, apricot, chocolate, cream, red, and silver.

Cockapoos whose coats are curly, like that of a poodle, may need trimming.

SIZES

A cockapoo's size is based on the size of its poodle parent. Cockapoos can weigh anywhere from less than 12 pounds (5 kg) to more than 20 pounds (9 kg)! However, most cockapoos fall into one of three groups.

Standard cockapoos stand more than 19 inches (48 cm) tall. They weigh 30 pounds (14 kg) or more. Miniature standard cockapoos are between 15 and 19 inches (38 and 48 cm) tall. They weigh between 20 and 30 pounds (9 and 14 kg).

Miniature cockapoos are just 10 to 15 inches (25 to 38 cm) tall. They weigh between 10 and 20 pounds (5 and 9 kg).

Cockapoo **breeders** make sure that the mother is the larger of the two parent dogs. If the mother is smaller than the father, she can have trouble giving birth to the puppies. Cockapoo puppies are born about 63 days after their parents mate.

Cockapoos are born blind and deaf. They will need to stay with their mother for ten weeks. Then, the puppies will be ready for a good home and a loving family!

CARE

The cockapoo's long, floppy ears are more likely to get infected than other types of dog ears. Professional dog groomers can help by shaving hair in and around the ears. And, a veterinarian can show owners how to keep their dogs' ears clean.

Cockapoos should visit a veterinarian once a year. The veterinarian will vaccinate them against common canine diseases. Unless the owners want to **breed** cockapoos, their dogs should be **spayed** or **neutered**.

Veterinarians will also watch for certain health problems that are common in cocker spaniels and poodles. The most common cockapoo problems include eye diseases, such as **cataracts**. Hip problems can be a concern, too.

Cockapoo owners should provide their dogs with fresh water and a healthy diet each day. They also need to make time to play with and exercise their dogs.

An owner who loves and cares for her cockapoo will have a loyal friend for 12 to 15 years.

GLOSSARY

American Kennel Club (AKC) - an organization that studies and promotes interest in purebred dogs.

breed - a group of animals sharing the same appearance and characteristics. A breeder is a person who raises animals. Raising animals is often called breeding them.

cataract - a clouding of the lens of the eye. This condition obstructs the passage of light through the eye and can result in blindness.

dander - saliva that dries on the skin or the coat when dogs groom themselves.

family - a group that scientists use to classify similar plants or animals. It ranks above a genus and below an order.

game - wild animals hunted for food or sport.

mellow - pleasant and agreeable.

muzzle - an animal's nose and jaws.

neuter - to remove a male animal's reproductive organs.

purebred - an animal whose parents are both from the same breed.

spay - to remove a female animal's reproductive organs.

unique - being the only one of its kind.

WEB SITES

To learn more about designer dogs, visit ABDO Publishing Company on the World Wide Web at **www.abdopublishing.com**. Web sites about designer dogs are featured on our Book Links page. These links are routinely monitored and updated to provide the most current information available.

23

INDEX

A
allergies 16
American Kennel
    Club 6, 8

B
breeders 6, 8, 10,
    12, 13, 18

C
Canidae 4
character 7, 9, 10,
    14, 15
coat 7, 12, 15, 16
cocker spaniel 5, 6,
    7, 10, 11, 20
color 12, 16

D
dander 16

E
ears 7, 12, 20
England 6
exercise 21
eyes 12, 20

F
food 21

G
genes 13, 16
grooming 12, 16,
    20

H
health 12, 13, 20
history 4, 6, 8, 10
hunting 4, 6, 8

K
Kennel Club 6

L
legs 12

M
mating 19
muzzle 12

N
neuter 20

P
poodle 5, 8, 9, 10,
    16, 18, 20
puppies 12, 13, 14,
    19
purebred 5, 12, 13

S
shedding 15, 16
size 6, 8, 18, 19
spay 20

T
tail 12
training 7, 9, 15

U
United States 7

V
veterinarian 20

W
water 21
wolf 4
working 8, 15